My Boss is a Jerk

How to Survive and Thrive in a Difficult Work Environment under the Control of a Bad Boss

By Kathleen Rao

Table of Contents

Introduction

Many employees can attest that having a mean boss absolutely makes their working environment intolerable. Tyrannical bosses are a huge pain when they consider themselves to be superior to their employees. They may even consider their employees to be not human, or unequal, in a sense, and therefore feel justified to treat them as such. They increase stress in the workplace that usually ends up affecting other spheres of your life.

For some of employees in this situation, their purpose in life becomes to look for another job. The assumption is that the new job they are dreaming of does not have a jerk for a boss. For some unexplainable reasons, the dreams of some individuals come true while others remain stuck in this difficult situation. This book will offer you some assistance in surviving in this type of difficult work environment ruled by a tyrannical boss. It will start by explaining how the tyrannical boss can be a hindrance to success, and will help you to comprehend the tyrannical boss's true personality. It will also show you how you can still thrive while working with this type of boss, and will demonstrate how you can sometimes even benefit from these bosses.

This book also explains why you should avoid quitting your job just because you have a tyrannical boss, especially if it's a job you want to (or need to) keep for certain reasons.

Chapter 1: Characteristics of a Tyrannical Boss

For an employee to understand their tyrannical boss and work effectively with them, it is important that the employee first become familiar with their character. You must become able to know how to avoid any humiliation that could emerge from a tyrannical boss's leadership, thus ensuring that you'll be free from any conflict that may come up as a result of interacting with such a boss. These are some characteristic of tyrannical bosses.

A Tyrannical boss acts childishly

The way a boss behaves is no different from that of a child. For example, the way they might express their displeasure with your work could be exhibited similar to a child's act of pouting or stomping their feet, or throwing a fit, figuratively speaking. Some of these bosses find it difficult to moderate their power and position at the workplace in an adult-like manner.

A Tyrannical boss is afraid and insecure

A tyrannical boss is often quite afraid of revealing the slightest bit of incompetence. The boss's mind is not always at peace when faced with certain difficult questions, especially if it is expected that someone in his position should know the answer. Almost all tyrannical bosses tend to seem to frequently get distracted or sidetracked, as a mechanism to dodge certain questions, regardless of the kind that you are working with.

A Tyrannical boss is selfish

Most of tyrannical bosses work hard to ensure that their workers do not significantly improve their own lifestyle because of the fear that their employees will be better than them and potentially threaten their position in some way. They give their workers a lot of work, but often underpay them to ensure that the employees are vulnerable to manipulation. Their focus is mainly based on improving their own living standards. They also think more highly of themselves than their workers.

A Tyrannical boss is a dictator

Tyrannical bosses do not respect or recognize the human rights or civil rights of employees. Workers do not have a say in determining who will be their boss, nor do they have a say in what tasks or projects they may be assigned. Yet more often than not, these bosses want their employees to worship and respect them.

A Tyrannical boss is egocentric

A self-centered boss doesn't work with the vision of the company in mind. Furthermore, he will avoid or despise workers who are of great importance and necessity to the company, in ensuring that the vision of the company is met.

A Tyrannical boss Withholds Praise

A tyrannical boss refuses to recognize his workers, even when they have improved their performance, done something great, or exceeded a certain expectation or milestone. This makes it difficult for some workers to advance in the organization, if promotions are based on performance reviews from your direct superior or boss. If you want to be at peace with your boss, you are supposed to play second fiddle – permanently.

Evaluating the characteristics of your boss will help you get clear with the fact that the problems you're experiencing at work really aren't caused by you at all. They're caused by the basic personality traits of your terrible boss. This basic understanding will help you to 'thicken your skin' so you won't mistake their issues with yours, and so you will be less offended by their behaviors. Once employees understand their boss's different character traits, it becomes easier to understand them and work with them (or around them). This will put you in a position of working with the boss with less conflict, and you'll earn respect from both the boss and from colleagues.

Chapter 2: Why it's Difficult to Work under the Control of a Bad Boss

There are a number of reasons employees don't like working with a tyrannical boss. One of them is that this type of boss frequently doesn't give their employees time or room to explain themselves in the case of anything going wrong. They try to make employees feel that they are the cause of the problem, or that at the very least they should have been able to prevent the problem. In many cases, workers become afraid of communicating with their boss because the boss is always unappreciative of them. They never take advice from their employees and they think that they are always right, even when they are wrong.

There are also some tyrannical bosses who will only notice and comment on the negative things that their employees have done, and they will never compliment them for any good work. Consequently, working with this type of boss creates quite a bit of insecurity, since the employee feels as if they may lose his or her job on the simple basis of the boss's moods. This generates tension for the workers while they are trying to perform their jobs.

Some of the tyrannical bosses do not allow their employees to take breaks, and they may even go to the extent of not paying the workers properly (wage theft). Most tyrannical bosses do more talking or procrastinating than actual work; they burden their employees with lots of work as they sit back in their offices drinking coffee and waiting for an occasion to scold their employees. They take credit for a job well done, while that credit really belongs to the employees.

Generally, the negative behavior from a boss like this really undermines the system of trust needs to be established between a boss and employee for the office and everyone in it to achieve its full potential. Some people actually become ill, physically or mentally, from the stress and frustration of working with this kind of boss.

Many people in this situation have the option to leave this type of job and go work elsewhere. However, if you took the job in the first place, you must have done it because it has something to offer that you believe other jobs don't. It could be that the job pays well and you need the money. Or it could be that the job offers a certain learning or training opportunity that will benefit your career in the long haul. So, if you'd really rather not leave your job, then keep reading.

Chapter 3: Common Symptoms and Consequences

There are lots of common symptoms that occur from working with a tyrannical boss. Some of these consequences include:

Stress: Employees who work with this kind of boss are frequently victims of a lot of stress, which leads to plenty of frustration, both while at the office and later at home, even in the evenings and on weekends. Sometimes people in this situation will even unintentionally take out their frustration on their family and loved ones.

Health problems: Your health is also at stake with this kind of leadership at work. An employee can suffer from heart problems or high blood pressure due to stress at the work place.

Economic problems and Job Insecurity: An employee can also suffer from economic problems as he or she tries to deal with the leadership at work. The boss can effectively decide to decrease your salary, or even fire you, whenever he or she pleases. Also the mental de-motivation that comes from working with a tyrannical boss often leads to a lack of motivation at work, which further leads to not doing such a good job, which leads to bad work, which leads to further criticism and risk of being fired or having your salary reduced. It's a downward spiral.

Emotional strain: Working with a tyrannical boss can cause an employee to suffer from massive amounts of emotional strain, due to in part to the verbal or even passive-aggressive abuse that may come from the boss. Some people even lose their self-esteem entirely.

Fatigue: When working with a tyrannical boss, you can be sure that you will be overworked, since the tyrannical boss assumes that others are machines and he is the only human being. This causes many employees come home from work feeling exhausted.

Lack of appreciation: In most cases, the employees of the tyrant are consistently unmotivated due to the boss's ignorance or lack of appreciation. The employees never know whether or not they are progressing.

Lack of confidence: Meeting with the boss is difficult because the boss looks down on the employees. The employees will then lack confidence in facing the boss whenever they need to address an issue directly with him or her. This also makes it tremendously more difficult in finding a new job because you don't feel confident enough to even apply to a new position, or confident enough to express your qualifications during an interview.

Chapter 4: How to Survive and Thrive!

Complaining about how tyrannical your boss is doesn't solve anything. Complaining can only result in making the situation worse and generating bitterness. Not getting along with your boss can also reflect negatively on your performance as an employee. Therefore, it is important that you work seriously on finding a way to get along with your boss. Doing so will help you in ensuring that you develop your career skills and objectives (the reason you have this job in the first place!).

The fact that you work with a tyrannical boss does not give you the freedom to hate your job since whatever brought you to that company has some significance. The following are some things that can be important in ensuring that you not only survive, but actually thrive, while working with a tyrannical boss.

Be proactive in a reactive work environment: if you are flexible, you will find it easy to work consistently all day. As an employee, be proactive about getting your next assignment, and the next one, and the next one, and schedule your work to avoid or reduce working in frenetic spurts. Instead of allowing others to dictate your schedule, make your work more manageable by keeping your own deadlines in mind. You'll be one step ahead at all times and your boss will be in less of a position to criticize. Make an effort to volunteer for new tasks as early as possible to minimize unexpected emergencies.

Find a good mentor: Remember you're not limited to getting advice only from the boss. Rather, take the time to find a person who can be trusted as a mentor. This could be someone at a different office, or department, or someone within your own office that has more experience.

Be a good mentor: Remind yourself that you have coworkers, some possibly younger or with less experience, that also work for this same Tyrant. Be a mentor to them. Knowing that they may be experiencing the same negative behavior from the boss, find little ways to make their day in the office somehow just a little bit better.

Be straightforward: It may help to be upfront, to the point, and avoid making small talk with your boss. Even your emails to your boss should be kept short and straight to the point.

Stay busy and remember why you're there: By keeping busy with your work, and staying focused on the task at hand, you'll have less time to spend focusing on or thinking about your boss's bad attitude and management style. Remember why you came to work there in the first place. Was it to learn something in particular? What task can you take on next that will improve your skillset or resume? Or do you want to build a network of colleagues that you'll keep in touch with and do business with years to come even when you move on past this job? Remember that they see your attitude and behavior too, so try to act with the utmost level of self-respect and self-reverence, even if your boss does put you in a bad mood. Don't let your boss have so much power over your mood that it affects the way others perceive you.

Make quick decisions: If your boss has the ability to make quick decisions, you as an employee have to work at the same pace as the boss because failure to do so can be perceived as inefficient, indecisive and slow. If you are the type of person who analyzes everything before speaking, try to anticipate questions that may be asked, and prepare your responses in advance.

Don't take things personally: Keep in mind that you do not need to be friends with the boss; all you have to do is to work together. There are lots of people in the world you won't get along with, or who might not think you're awesome. So try not to let it get to you. You've got friends and family at home who love and adore you. Who cares what this jerk thinks?

Chapter 5: Benefits of Having a Good Relationship with Your Boss

Like it or not, a good relationship with your boss really is critical to your success in the workplace. This is something that will not only make your job easier, but you will also enjoy going to work every day, and you will continue to advance your career.

Your boss has a big impact on your success or failure at work, so developing a good relationship with him or her is a good way to progress in the workplace. Since the boss is the one with the final say in the office, working under him can become unbearable if you do not have a good relationship. So, as an employee, you should strive to have a good relationship with both your employer and your colleagues. In order for you to have a good relationship with your boss, there are some factors that you need to take into account. They include:

Meeting your Boss's needs before he asks:

From the first day of employment, your mission should be to find and meet the needs of your boss. By doing so, you will have taken a major step in establishing a good relationship. It does not matter how old you are; what matters is your ability to manage your boss and this can be done by delivering what your boss requires before he or she asks for it. Don't wait for your boss to tell you what to do. Make his or her job easier and impress him or her by taking the initiative in doing things you need to do without being asked.

Schedule Meetings with your Boss:

It is advisable to set time for meetings with your boss when you see that things are not going well in your organization. Be brief when presenting your case. Meet regularly with your boss not only to talk about problems but also to give him or her updates on how things are going in the organization. You can use this time to update your boss about your projects and your accomplishments and also to get your questions answered. Meeting your deadlines is very important; you cannot expect to have a good relationship with your boss if you are not performing up to what is expected from you. You can be the proactive one, and initiate these pow-wows to show that you care and are really trying to do a good job.

You need to be friendly:

To have a good relationship with your boss you have to show friendliness. Friendliness makes it easier to establish a comfortable working relationship. Friendliness is not the same as being Friends. You don't have to be friends with your boss.

Help your boss look great:

Ensuring that your manager looks good is one of the best things you can do to improve or strengthen your relationship. When your organization succeeds, it reflects well upon your boss and you, and is ultimately good for your career. Find ways for your skills to complement those of your boss, so that you can help your boss succeed as well.

Avoid gossip:

Gossip can hurt your relationship with your boss. Avoid talking negatively about your boss to your colleagues, because if this reaches him you will find yourself in a lot of trouble.

Chapter 6: How to Keep Your Job While Dealing With a Bad Boss

Most employees do not want to lose their jobs in spite of the fact that they are working for a tyrannical boss. However, for you to successfully keep your job while working with a tyrannical boss, it is important that you should familiarize yourself with these six things. They are of great importance in ensuring that you keep your job.

Identify the boss's key priorities and make sure that you assist him in fulfilling them.

Unless you help the tyrannical boss fulfill his priorities, this type of boss will never open up and become receptive to you. The boss will find it easier to respond to the needs of the employees and respect them if they are working hard to ensure that his own priorities are met.

You should know how to be useful to the boss beyond your normal duties or responsibilities.

If you become indispensable, the boss will consistently ask for your assistance and will ultimately appreciate you. Working beyond your normal responsibilities will make tyrannical bosses soften their approach to you. Moreover, they will appreciate the kind of service that you offer them, as an employee in their company who's helping him reach his goals.

Learn how to neutralize the boss's emotional reaction when he is critical.

You need to get to know, and anticipate, your boss's triggers. You've probably already done this, and you generally know when one of his tirades or pout-fests is headed your way. Try out different responses, and see how he reacts to different ones. Which one best neutralizes his position? Make a list of options, and for the next few times he attacks you with criticism, try each one until you've tried them all. Here are some examples. Option A) you defend yourself, verbally trying to explain why you did what you did and why you thought it was best given the scenario. Option B) you apologize immediately, express your understanding of his concern, and come up with a creative suggestion how to remedy the situation. Option C) you politely, but sternly, say to your boss that you don't feel comfortable with the way he's speaking to you, and that you'd be glad to discuss it with him if he wants to do it calmly and in a positive problem-solving manner. These are just examples, but by trying a few out and observing your boss's reaction, you will ultimately get a feel for what type of response can neutralize him quickest.

Empower yourself in all areas:

If you do not empower yourself in every aspect of your life, someone else will be the one with power over you. Reducing the chance of being bullied in the workplace is dependent on how you invest in your life in terms of education, communication skills, self-worth and self-image. You should expand your knowledge in everything that you do to avoid being manipulated or bullied. Even things entirely unrelated to the workplace will help build your confidence and make you feel empowered. Working out to become more fit or lose some weight, for example, will ultimately lead to a more-confident-You when you're at work.

Grow from the experience, and take some control over how you perceive it.

How you perceive your experience and how you act are the most important things happening within any experience. You should be a master of your own destiny. Decide the kind of life that you want to live and how you want to interact with your boss, to avoid becoming a victim of your own story. If that means standing up for yourself, great. If that means just trying not to take anything he says personally, great. But whatever you decide, take control of your own response mechanism.

Be honest with your Boss.

Sometimes, tyrannical bosses do not know the impact of their actions. Be aware of any opportunity to share with the boss how both his leadership and actions affect your working relationship. Do this with a lot of humility and let the boss see how serious you are while confronting him in a polite way. Do not do this in public as it can damage the reputation of both the boss and employee. Make sure that the way you communicate with the boss is compelling while presenting your thoughts in a way that they cannot be turned against you.

Conclusion

Thank you for purchasing this book! I really hope it helped you better understand the mentality of your Boss, and the reason he acts the way he does. Remember, it's your boss's own personality flaw and insecurities, and therefore any criticism from this boss does not represent your worth as a person or as an employee. Adapting a different attitude based on this understanding will help you begin to have a stress-free work environment and relationship with your boss.

You will be in a better position to keep your job and focus on the reason you starting working there in the first place, despite the challenges you face when working for a tyrannical boss. The more you empower yourself and take control of your own responses, the more confident you'll be in general, and the stronger you'll be when interacting with such a terrible boss. Consequently, your boss will soften his approach to you and have more respect for you, thus making your work environment a little bit better and more tolerable.

Thanks again, and good luck! Oh also, if you enjoyed this book, please take the time to share your thoughts and post a review on Amazon. It'd be greatly appreciated!

59306428R00022